The Great National Health Colouring Book

Written & Illustrated by Diana Matos Gagic

**First published in 2021 by
Crafty Birdie Designs**

Text copyright © Diana Gagic, 2021
Illustrations copyright © Diana Gagic, 2021

Design for print by
Fullstop Studio

Edited & proofread by
Emma Turner
Carey Smith
John Whiteside

Created in Yorkshire

The moral right of Diana Gagic to be identified as the author and illustrator of this work has been asserted in accordance with Sections 77 and 78 of the Copyright, Designs and Patents Act 1988.

All rights reserved.
No part of this book may be reproduced, transmitted or stored in any form or by any means, graphic, electronic or mechanical, including photocopying, taping and recording, without prior written permission from the author and publisher.

email: craftybirdies@gmail.com
Etsy: CraftyBirdieDesigns

Printed in England

ISBN 978-1-9160072-7-7

The nation has been truly shaken by the worldwide Covid-19 crisis and those working on the frontline of health and social care have been particularly hard hit. Contained within these pages you'll find hand-drawn illustrations alongside written information on some of the many job roles encompassed within the health sector. The roles included here are by no means an exhaustive list, but rest assured, this book has been made with love as a tribute to all of our hardworking key workers.

This book has been made with responsibly sourced, uncoated paper.
It is suitable for colouring in using pens, pencils or crayons of your choosing...
so feel free to be as creative as you like!

Proudly supporting NHS Charities Together

For each copy sold by the publisher, £1 will be donated to NHS Charities Together
(registered charity no. 1186569).

About the Author / Illustrator

Diana was born in Halifax General Hospital, to Portuguese parents and has lived for many years in the beautiful Yorkshire village of Haworth. Drawing inspiration from a life-long love of the creative arts and learning, combined with an understanding of the importance of care for our physical and mental health, Diana has created this hand-illustrated book to celebrate our valued health service workers. It aims to honour the many hardworking individuals who dedicate their working lives to providing health and social care to the nation.

UK Healthcare

The UK's National Health Service was launched on 5th July 1948, with the aim of providing free healthcare at the point of use to all those in need. Aneurin Bevan, then Minister of Health for the Labour Government, and his wife, MP Jennie Lee, are attributed with being the key influencers in its founding. Today, it is the UK's largest employer, although many years of funding cuts, combined with growing demands for patient care have increased pressure on hardworking staff and services.

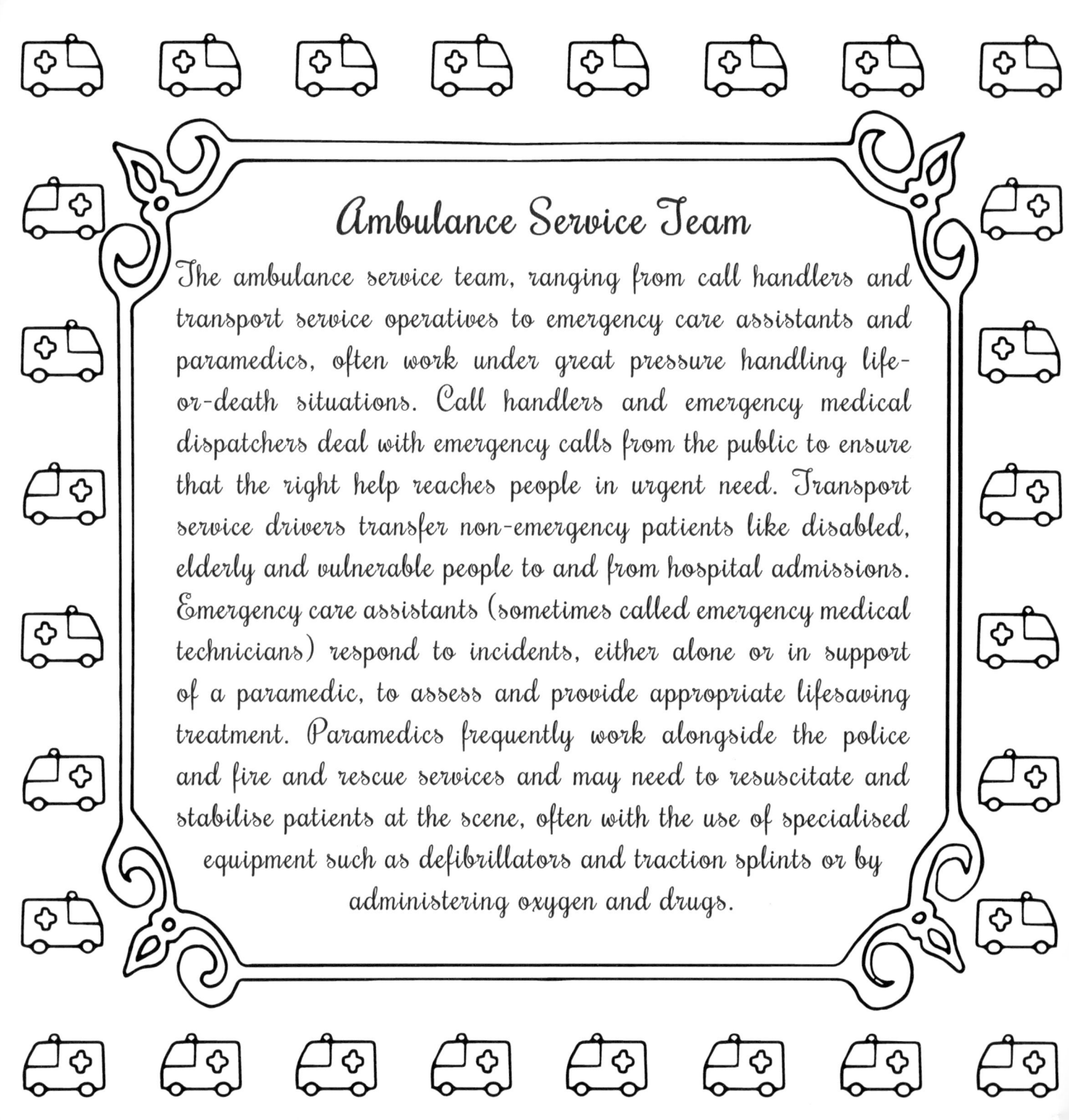

Ambulance Service Team

The ambulance service team, ranging from call handlers and transport service operatives to emergency care assistants and paramedics, often work under great pressure handling life-or-death situations. Call handlers and emergency medical dispatchers deal with emergency calls from the public to ensure that the right help reaches people in urgent need. Transport service drivers transfer non-emergency patients like disabled, elderly and vulnerable people to and from hospital admissions. Emergency care assistants (sometimes called emergency medical technicians) respond to incidents, either alone or in support of a paramedic, to assess and provide appropriate lifesaving treatment. Paramedics frequently work alongside the police and fire and rescue services and may need to resuscitate and stabilise patients at the scene, often with the use of specialised equipment such as defibrillators and traction splints or by administering oxygen and drugs.

Doctors

Medical doctors train as junior doctors to examine, diagnose and treat patients and can progress to become senior doctors and consultants within hospitals or as community based GPs (general practitioners). A doctor can specialise in many different areas of medicine such as: A&E (accident and emergency), anaesthesiology, cardiology, dermatology, endocrinology, gastroenterology, geriatrics, haematology, neurology, obstetrics, oncology, ophthalmology, paediatrics, pathology, psychiatry, radiology, nephrology, respiratory, rheumatology and reproductive health etc. A few of these specialist roles are included in the following pages although it is, unfortunately, not possible to pay tribute to every individual area here.

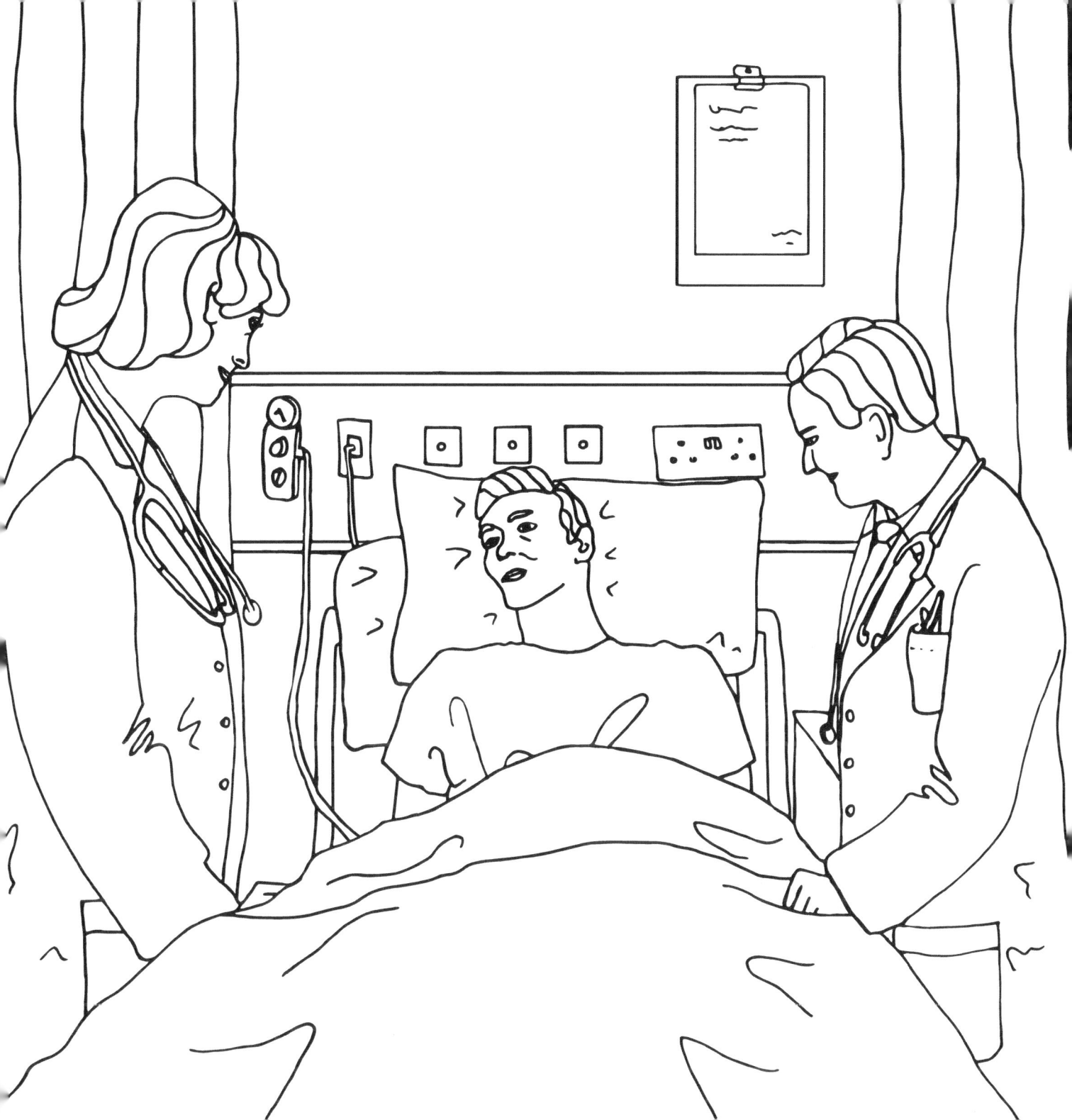

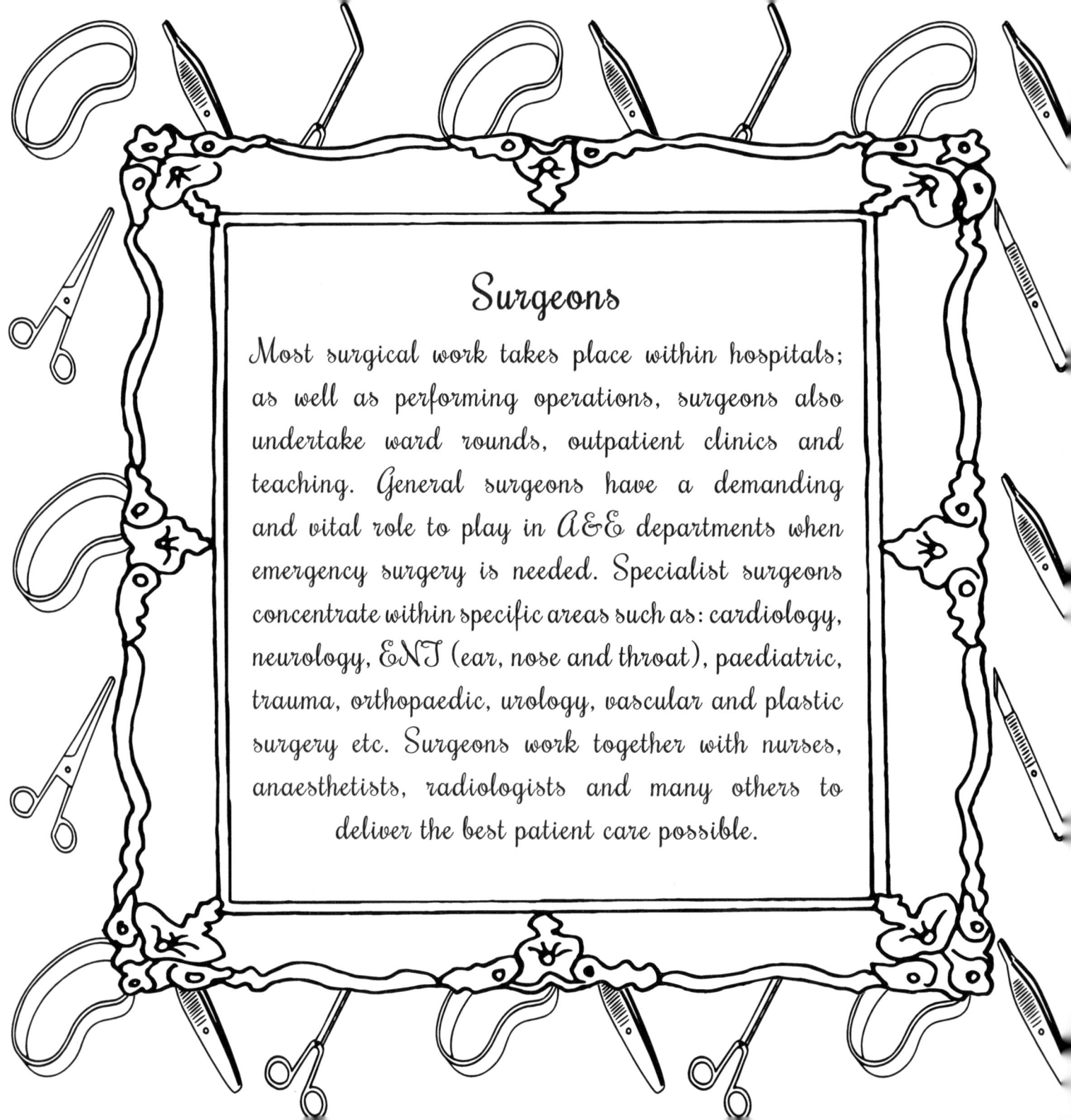

Surgeons

Most surgical work takes place within hospitals; as well as performing operations, surgeons also undertake ward rounds, outpatient clinics and teaching. General surgeons have a demanding and vital role to play in A&E departments when emergency surgery is needed. Specialist surgeons concentrate within specific areas such as: cardiology, neurology, ENT (ear, nose and throat), paediatric, trauma, orthopaedic, urology, vascular and plastic surgery etc. Surgeons work together with nurses, anaesthetists, radiologists and many others to deliver the best patient care possible.

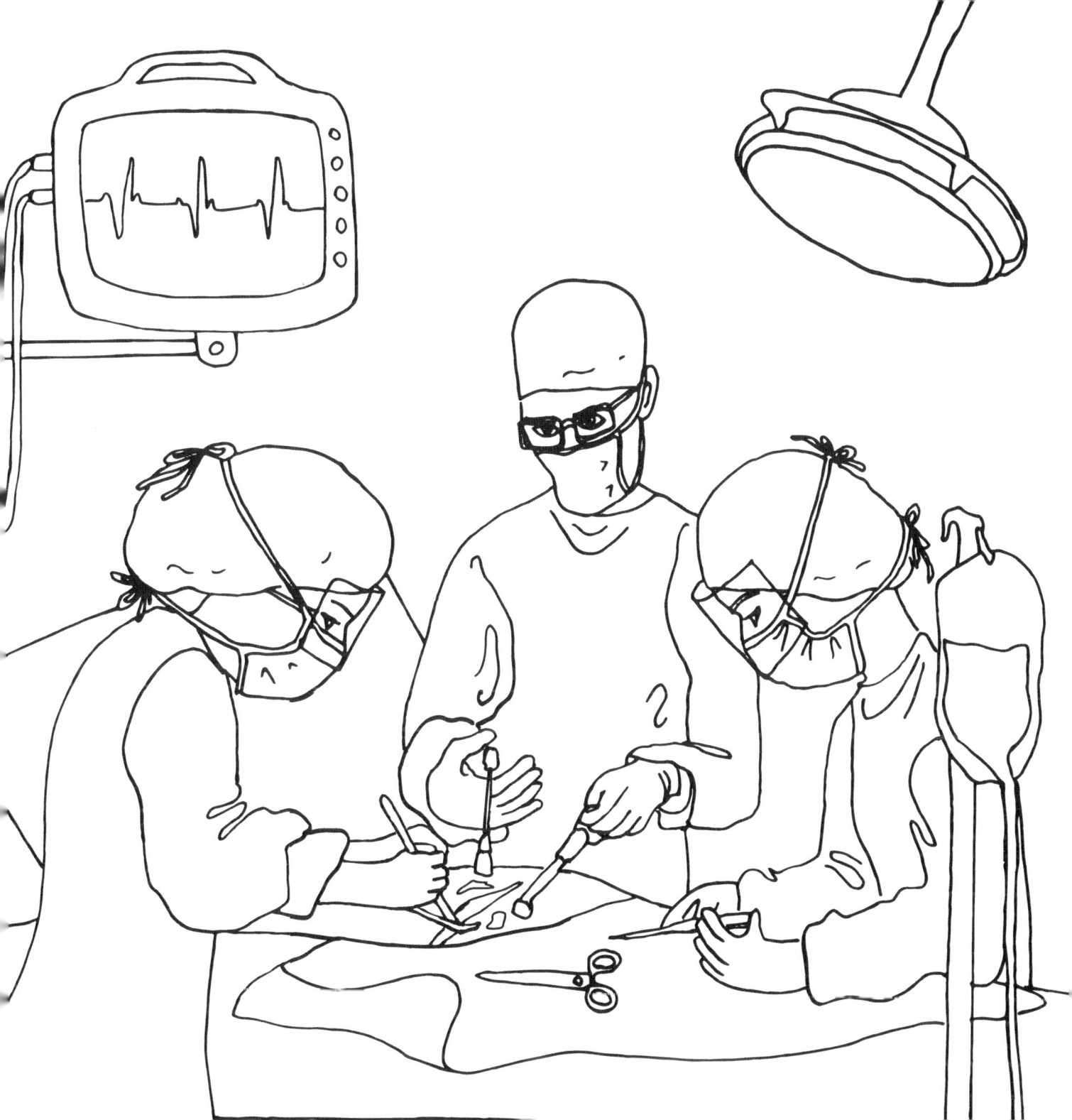

Nurses

Nurses are the hardworking backbone of our health system and there are over 500,000 nurses working in the UK. Florence Nightingale is regarded as the founder of the modern nursing profession having initiated formal schools of nursing in the late 19th and early 20th centuries. There are a multitude of essential nursing roles which cover four main fields: adult, child, mental health and learning disability. Nursing skills and responsibilities vary depending on the care setting but all practise the '6C' core values of care, compassion, courage, communication, commitment and competence. All nurses in the UK are registered with the Nursing and Midwifery Council.

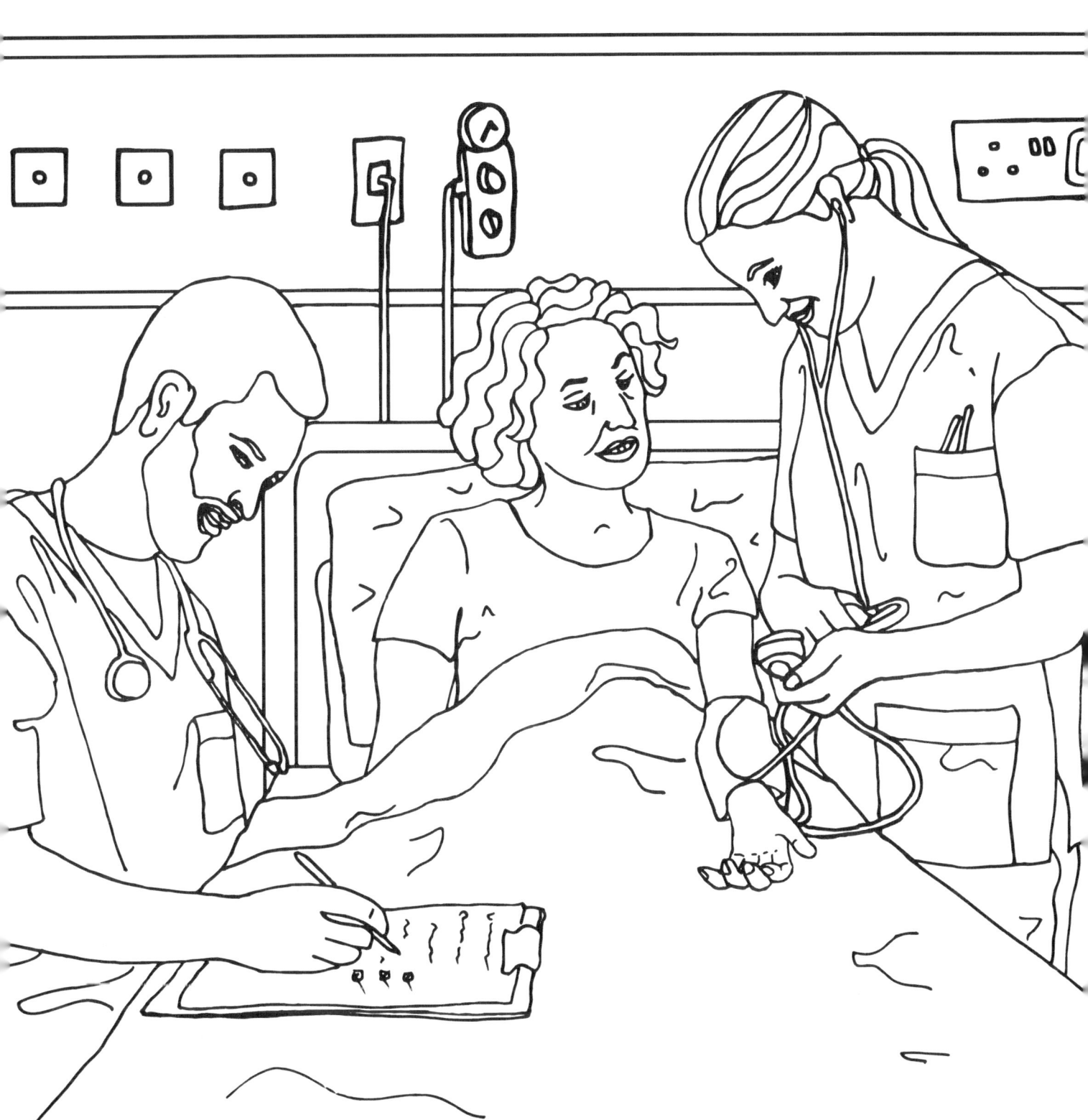

Midwifery

Midwives and midwifery assistants are experts on childbirth and are on the frontline of providing personal care for women throughout pregnancy, labour and the time shortly after birth. Within the UK, midwives work within a large multi-disciplinary team of health professionals including sonographers, obstetricians, anaesthetists and paediatricians to help women make informed choices about the best options and services available to them. The related role of a health visitor specialises in working with young families to help identify specific health and social needs to improve overall child health and wellbeing.

Cardiologists

Cardiologists are highly trained specialists who diagnose and assess treatment for patients with heart and blood vessel (cardiovascular system) problems. They make decisions about medications and surgery to help restore blood circulation. Cardiologists prescribe medicine and recommend healthy lifestyle habits such as eating a good diet, taking regular exercise and reducing stress levels to help improve and promote good heart health.

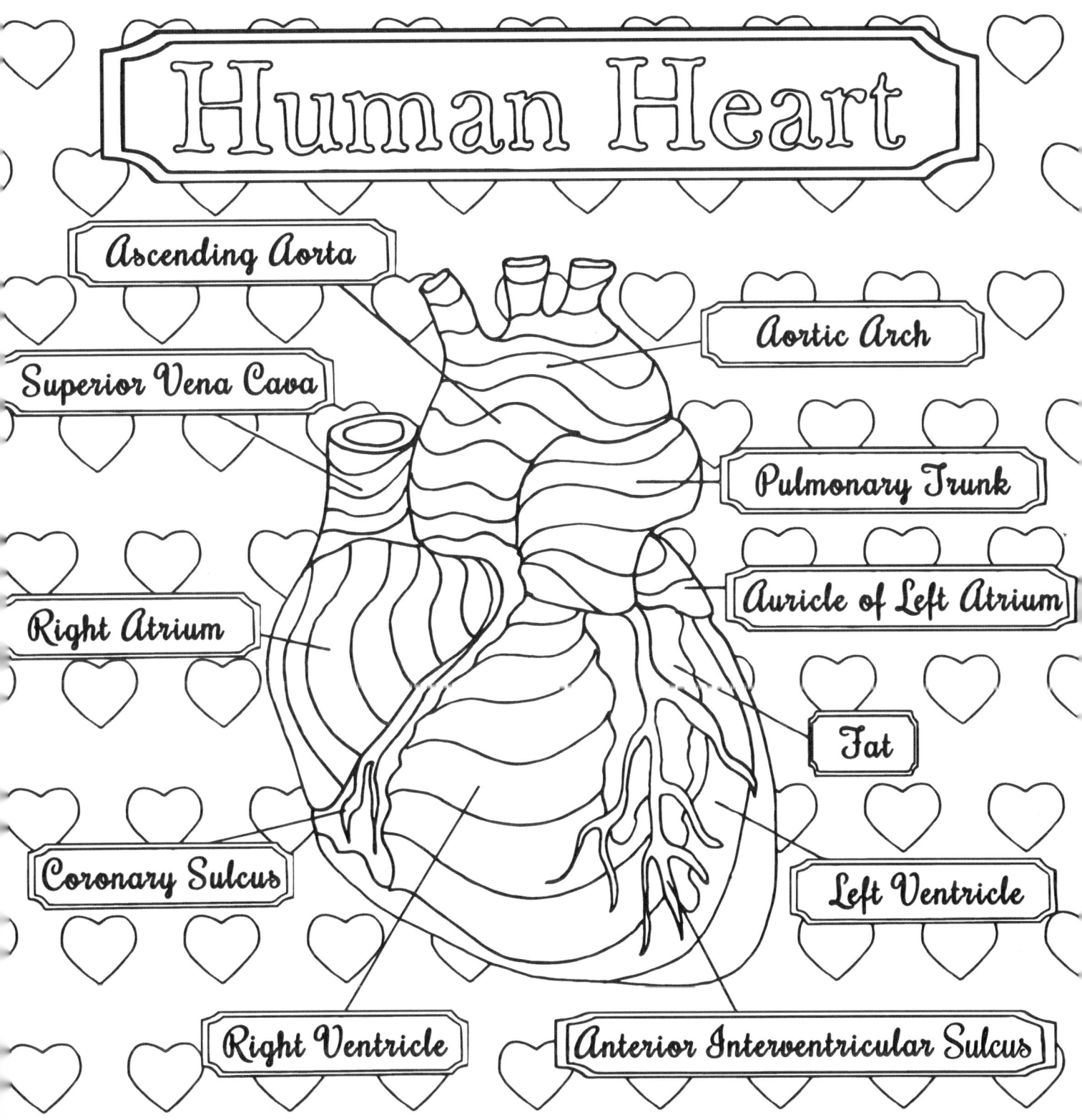

Radiologists

Radiologists are doctors who use images such as: X-rays, computed tomography (CT), magnetic resonance imaging (MRI), positron emission tomography (PET) and ultrasound to see what's going on inside a patient's body to help diagnose, treat and manage medical conditions and injuries. Radiologists work closely with radiographers who operate the machinery and perform the scans. The resulting images allow radiologists to analyse a wide range of conditions such as: blocked arteries, broken bones, pregnancy, joint injuries, foreign objects in the body etc.

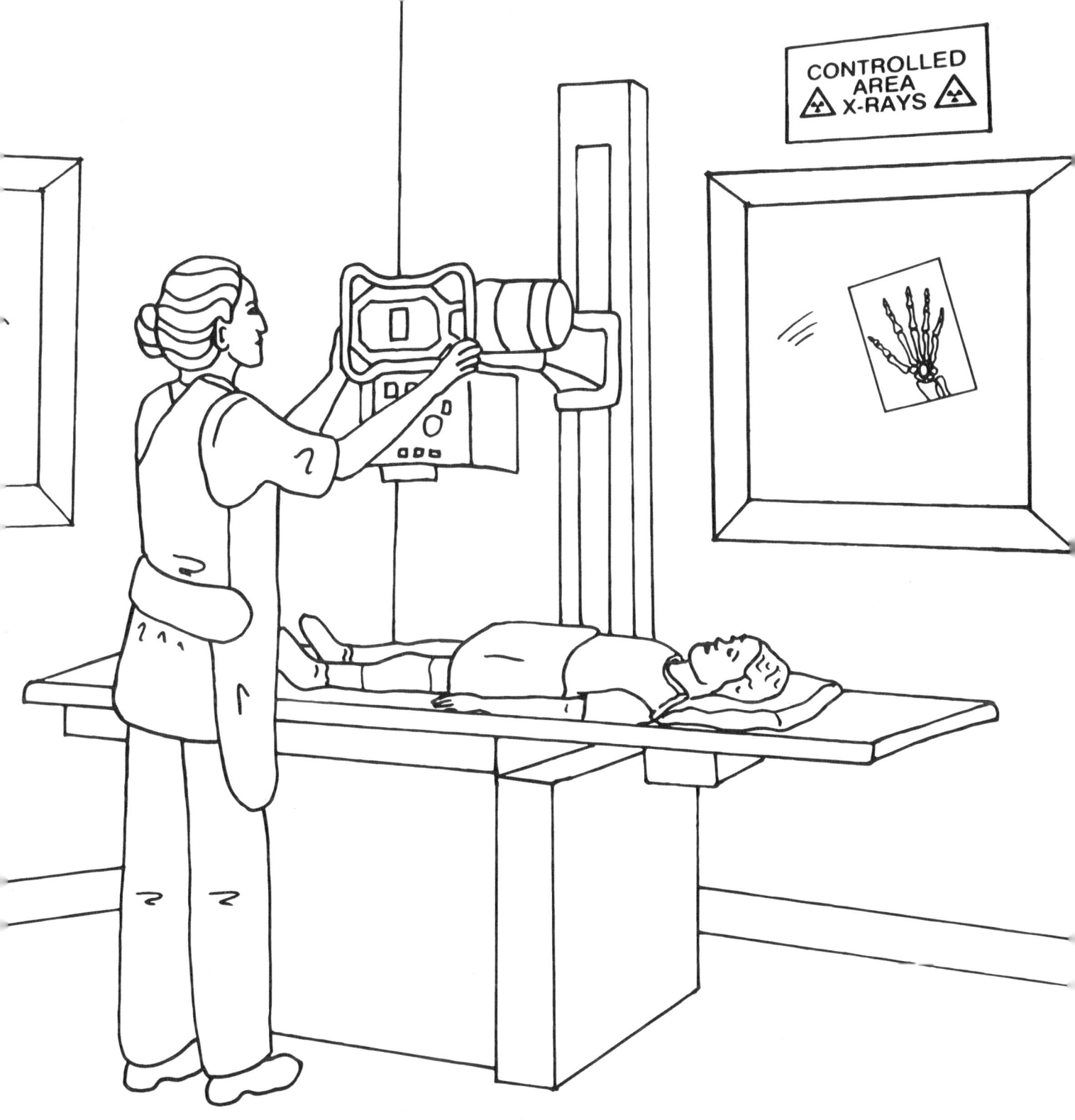

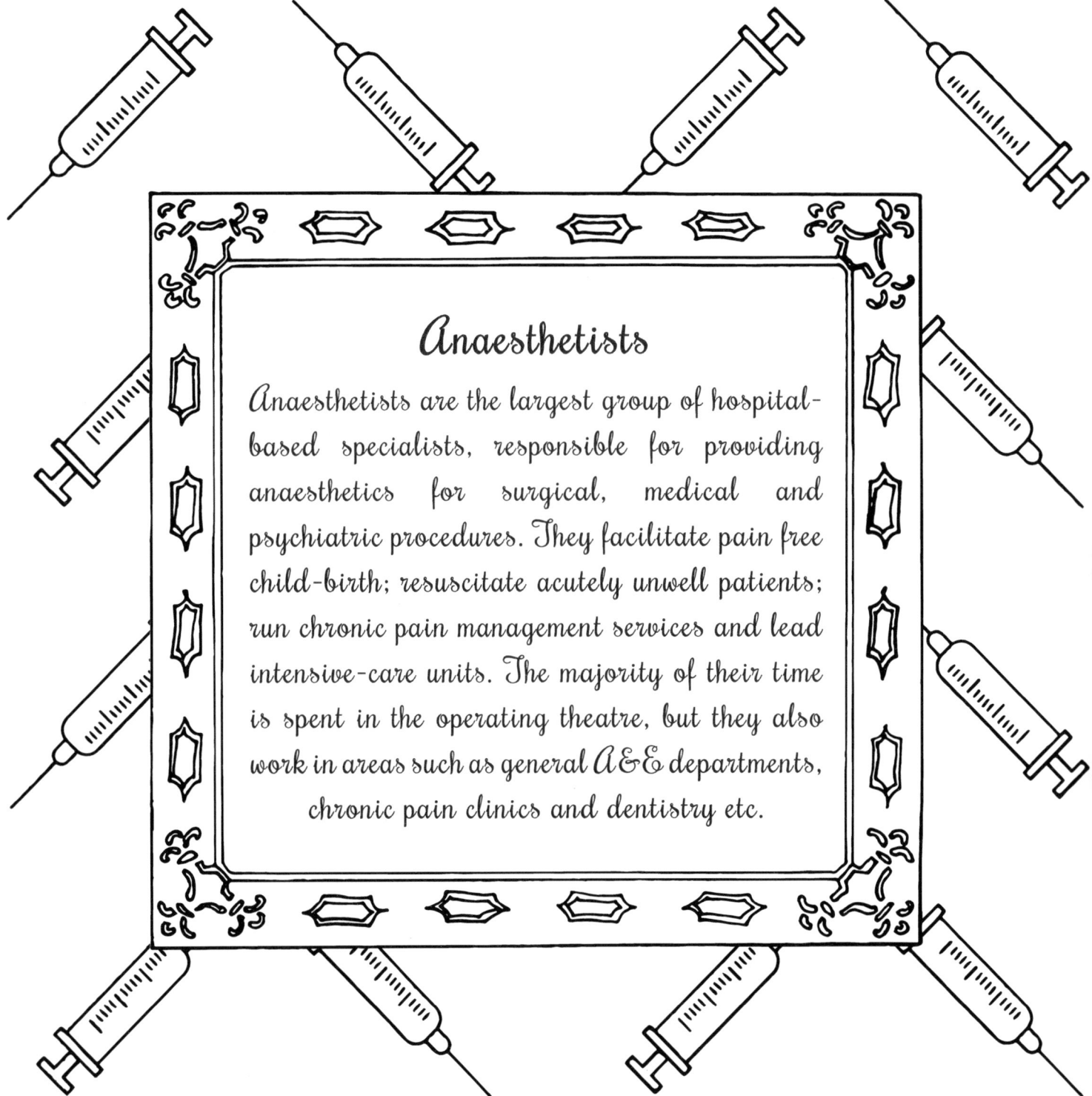

Anaesthetists

Anaesthetists are the largest group of hospital-based specialists, responsible for providing anaesthetics for surgical, medical and psychiatric procedures. They facilitate pain free child-birth; resuscitate acutely unwell patients; run chronic pain management services and lead intensive-care units. The majority of their time is spent in the operating theatre, but they also work in areas such as general A&E departments, chronic pain clinics and dentistry etc.

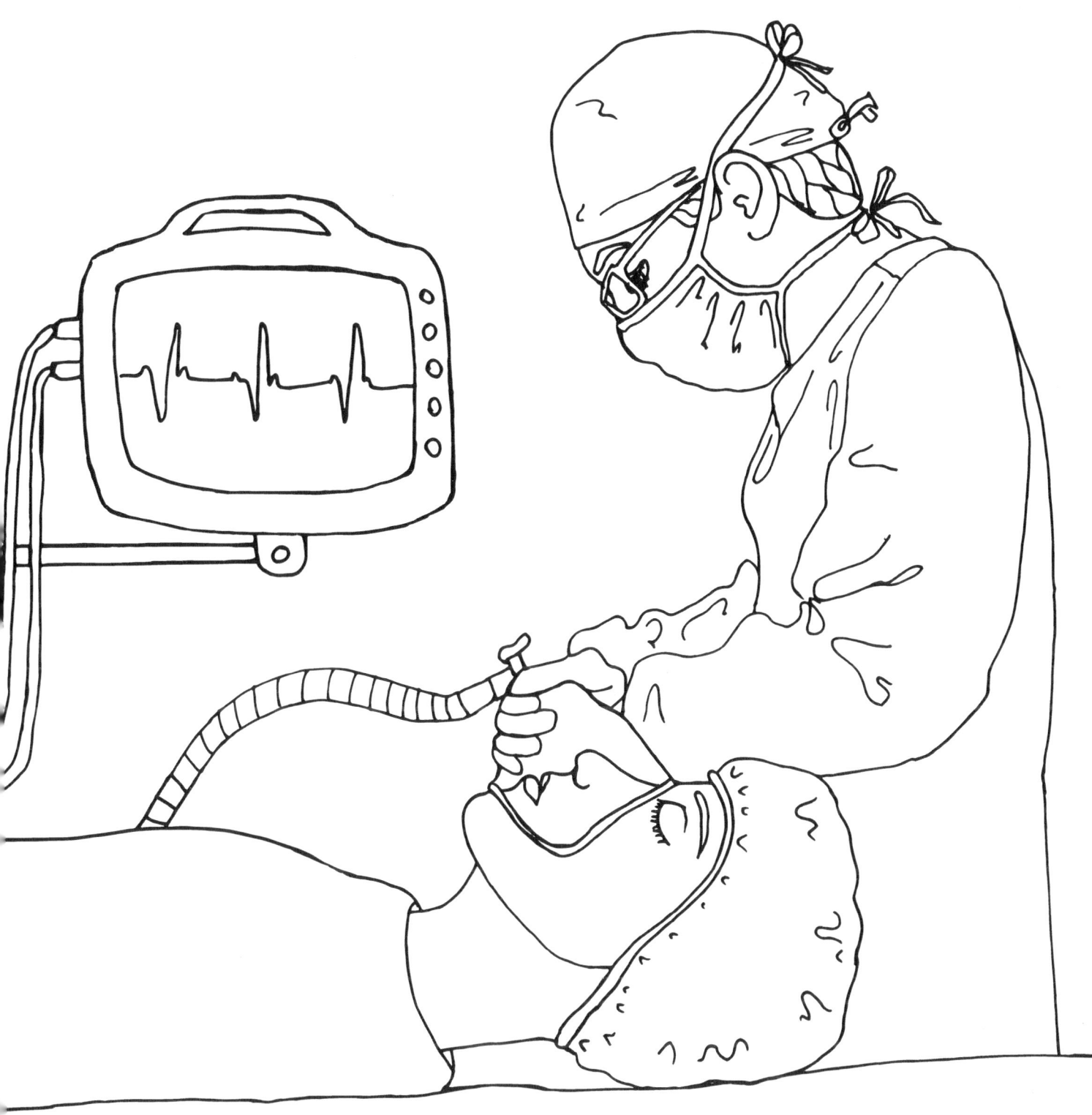

Psychiatrists

In today's modern world, the connection between stress and mental health is well known. There are a great many roles linked to the mental health services, including: psychiatrists, clinical psychologists, cognitive behavioural therapists (CBT), councillors, forensic psychologists, social workers and art therapists etc. Psychiatrists are qualified to prescribe medication as well as recommend other forms of treatment to help people with their mental health and linked behavioural problems. There are many mental health conditions that may be diagnosed and treated by a psychiatrist, such as: anxiety, phobias, obsessive-compulsive disorder (OCD), post-traumatic stress disorder (PTSD), personality disorders, schizophrenia and paranoia, depression and bipolar disorder, dementia and Alzheimer's disease, eating disorders, sleep disorders and addictions.

Ophthalmologists

Ophthalmologists are doctors/surgeons who are specially trained in eye care. They assess and treat eye conditions or diseases of the eye, and are qualified to prescribe medication and carry out surgery. Optometrists also examine and identify the signs of problems with vision and general health and can offer clinical advice regarding eye health and vision correction, prescribe spectacles or contact lenses and make referrals to see an ophthalmologist if required. An optician carries out general eye tests and supplies and fits glasses and contact lenses to correct vision. Whilst an optician is not an eye doctor, they are on the frontline of detecting and identifying the early stages of eye problems and some health conditions.

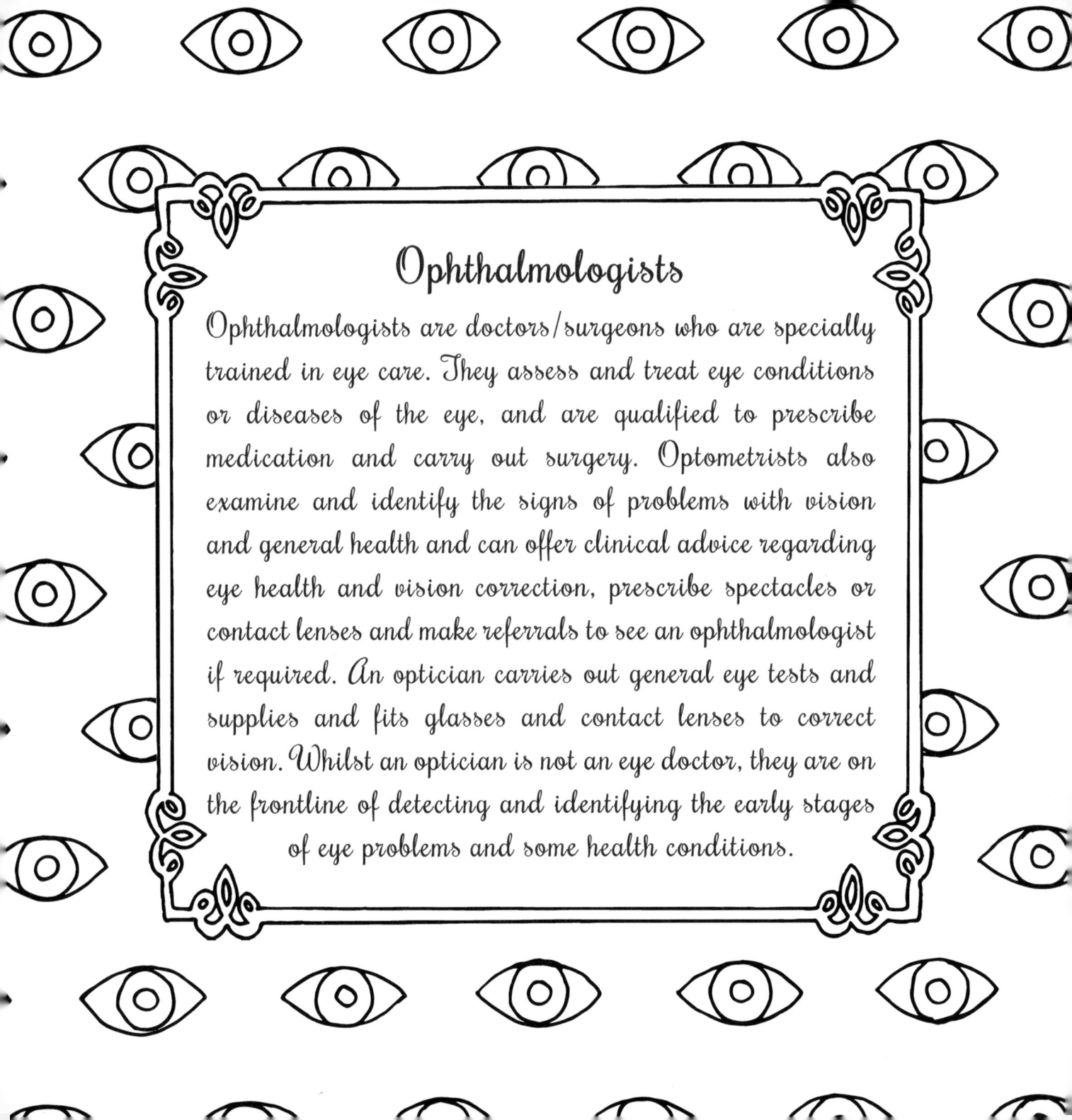

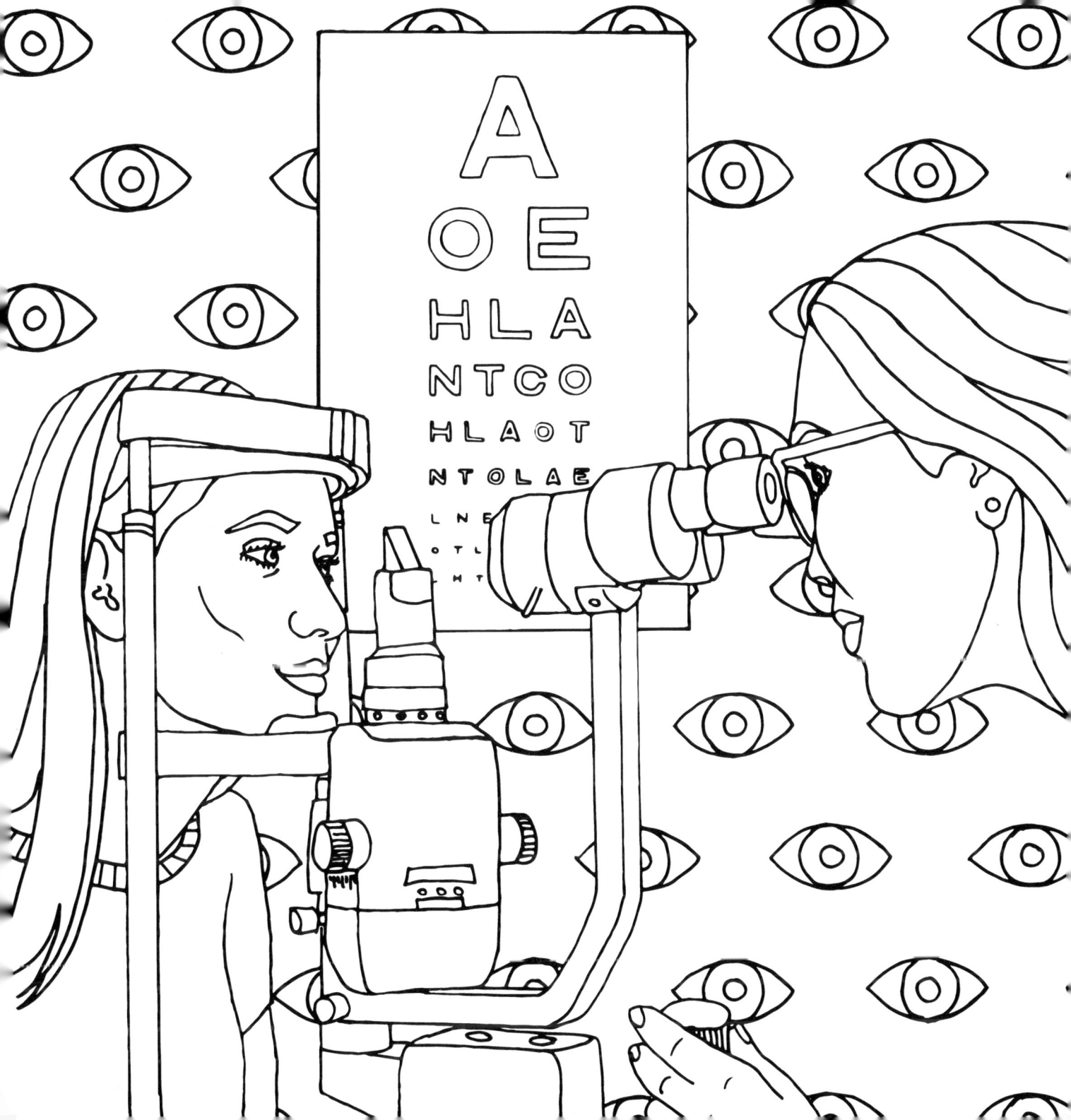

Biomedical Scientists

The scientific healthcare workforce is an essential part of our health services. Biomedical scientists carry out laboratory tests on bodily tissue and fluid samples in order to support the diagnosis and treatment of diseases. While people working in healthcare science make up only 5% of the total staff of the national health services, the majority of all health diagnoses are made using the test results provided by biomedical scientists. Every year, biomedical professionals carry out nearly 1 billion pathology laboratory tests!

Dental Practitioners

The dental team are on the frontline of good oral health, helping to prevent and treat dental and oral disease, correct dental irregularities and treat dental/facial injuries. The team consists of dentists, dental nurses, dental therapists, dental hygienists, dental technicians/technologists and orthodontists. Complex oral and maxillofacial surgery is carried out in hospitals but most dental care services are provided through high street practices. To a lesser degree, dental work is also carried out in a variety of other community settings such as in care homes, mobile clinics and within the army etc.

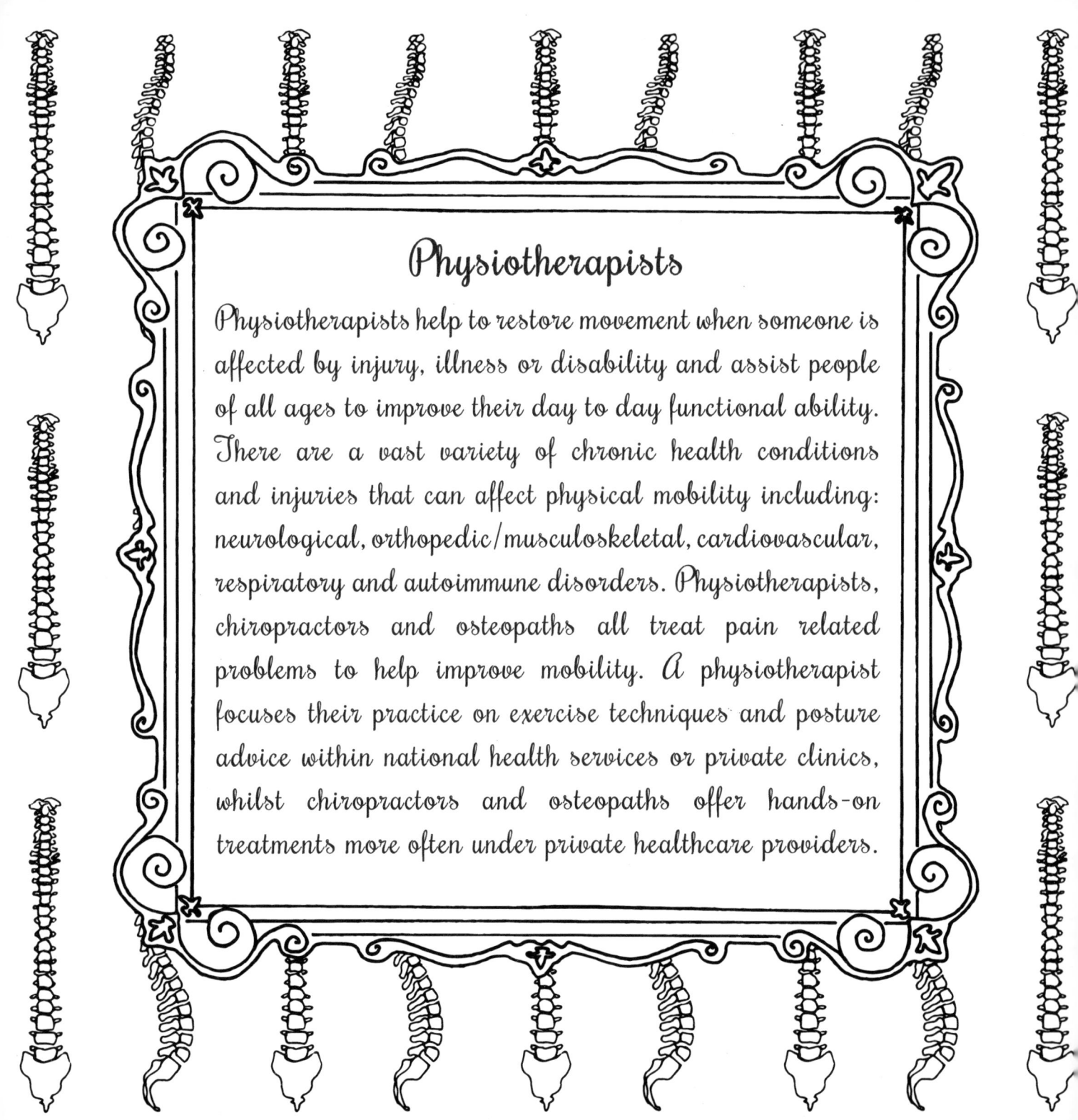

Physiotherapists

Physiotherapists help to restore movement when someone is affected by injury, illness or disability and assist people of all ages to improve their day to day functional ability. There are a vast variety of chronic health conditions and injuries that can affect physical mobility including: neurological, orthopedic/musculoskeletal, cardiovascular, respiratory and autoimmune disorders. Physiotherapists, chiropractors and osteopaths all treat pain related problems to help improve mobility. A physiotherapist focuses their practice on exercise techniques and posture advice within national health services or private clinics, whilst chiropractors and osteopaths offer hands-on treatments more often under private healthcare providers.

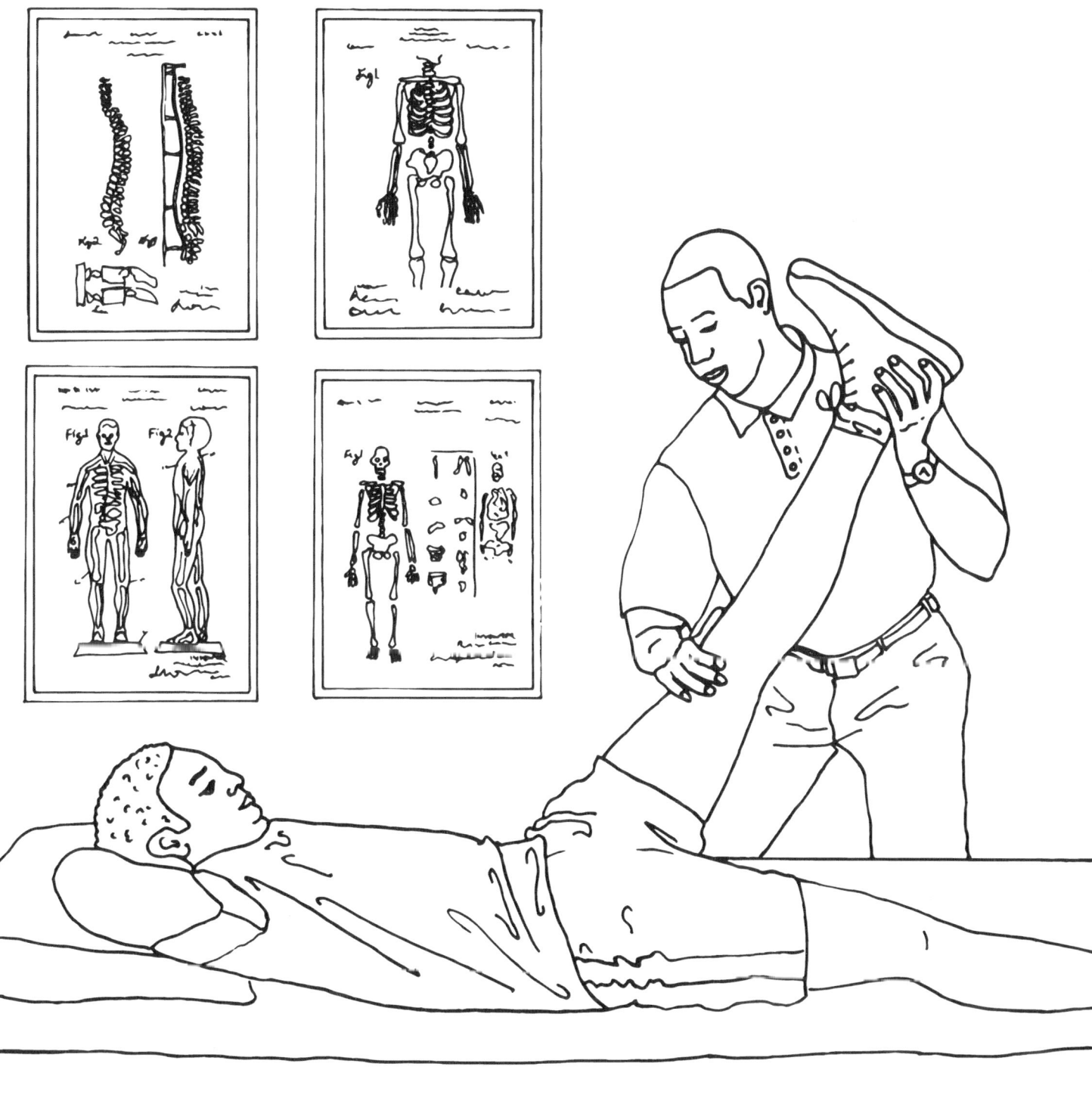

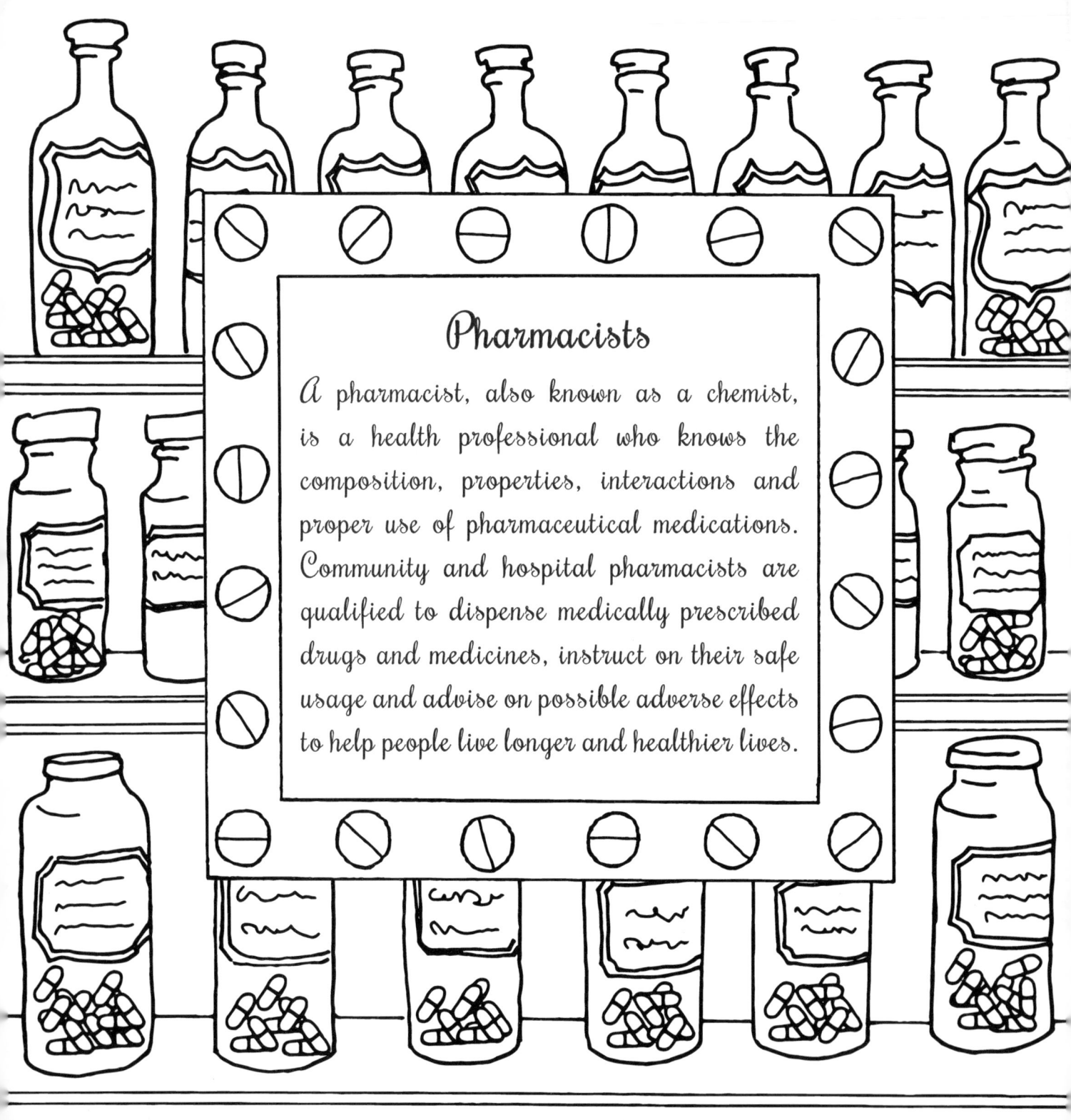

Pharmacists

A pharmacist, also known as a chemist, is a health professional who knows the composition, properties, interactions and proper use of pharmaceutical medications. Community and hospital pharmacists are qualified to dispense medically prescribed drugs and medicines, instruct on their safe usage and advise on possible adverse effects to help people live longer and healthier lives.

Social Workers

Community health services provide support to people of all ages, assisting individuals and their families with a variety of complex health and social needs. Poverty and mental health problems are closely interlinked and social work has its roots in the attempt to deal with the effects of inequality in society. Working in collaboration with other professionals in health, housing and employment etc, social work aims to support and empower vulnerable people, including those living with frailty or chronic conditions, to live their lives more successfully. Women perform around 90% of the direct care and support-providing job roles within social care.

Key Workers

This book is dedicated to our hardworking health service workers and it cannot go without a special mention to the cleaning and clerical teams who are essential to keeping our hospitals hygienic and organised. Thank you also to the many volunteers, unpaid carers and other key workers involved in keeping society functioning—all those involved in the production, sale and distribution of food and other necessary goods, energy, water and waste utilities, communication networks, postal services, transport services, education, media, finance, police and fire rescue etc. There are also many less obvious roles, such as those within the sports and creative arts industries, which, although not officially recognised as essential, prove to be invaluable in preventing illness by helping to reduce stress and maintaining overall health and wellbeing.

Keep creative and keep strong!